Simply Science

SIMPLE MACHINES

Discover Science Through Facts and Fun

By Steve Way and Gerry Bailey

Science and curriculum consultant:
Debra Voege, M.A., science curriculum resource teacher

Gareth Stevens
Publishing

Please visit our web site at www.garethstevens.com.
For a free catalog describing our list of high-quality books, call 1-800-542-2595 (USA)
or 1-800-387-3178 (Canada). Our fax: 1-877-542-2596

Library of Congress Cataloging-in-Publication Data

Way, Steve.
    Simple Machines/by Steve Way.
      p. cm.—(Simply Science)
    Includes bibliographical references and index.
    ISBN-10: 0-8368-9231-3   ISBN-13: 978-0-8368-9231-4 (lib. bdg.)
    1. Simple machines—Juvenile literature. I. Title.
TJ147.W39 2008
621.8—dc22   2008012425

This North American edition first published in 2009 by
Gareth Stevens Publishing
A Weekly Reader® Company
1 Reader's Digest Road
Pleasantville, NY 10570-7000 USA

This edition copyright © 2009 by Gareth Stevens, Inc. Original edition copyright © 2007 by
Diverta Publishing Ltd., First published in Great Britain by Diverta Publishing Ltd., London, UK.

Gareth Stevens Senior Managing Editor: Lisa M. Herrington
Gareth Stevens Creative Director: Lisa Donovan
Gareth Stevens Designer: Keith Plechaty
Gareth Stevens Associate Editor: Amanda Hudson
Special thanks to Mark Sachner

Photo Credits: Cover (t) The Car Photo Library, (b) Darin Mickey/Getty Images; p. 5 Maximilian
Stock Ltd/Science Photo Library; pp. 20-21 (t) The Car Photo Library, (l) The Motoring Picture Library,
(c) Auto Express Images, (r) Helen King/CORBIS; p. 22 Dorling Kindersley Images; p. 23 (t) Kennedy
Space Center/NASA, (l) Shutterstock, (b) Darin Mickey/Getty Images; p. 25 (t) Mixa/Getty Images, (b)
Ace Stock Ltd/Alamy; p. 26 Dorling Kindersley Images.

Illustrations: Steve Boulter and Xact Studio

Diagrams: Ralph Pitchford

Every effort has been made to trace the copyright holders for the photos used in this book, and
the publisher apologizes in advance for any unintentional omissions. We would be pleased to insert
the appropriate acknowledgements in any subsequent edition of this publication.

Printed in the United States of America

1 2 3 4 5 6 7 8 9 10 09 08

CONTENTS

What Is a Machine? 4

Six Simple Machines 6

The Pulley 8

The Lever 10

The Inclined Plane 12

The Screw 14

The Wedge 16

The Wheel and Axle 18

Simple Machines at Work 20

What Powers Machines? 22

Simple Machines in the Home 24

Two Machines Together 26

Fun with Simple Machines 28

Simple Machines Quiz 30

Glossary 31

Index 32

What Is a Machine?

Machines are things...
that **bang**
and **clank**
and **grind**
and **hiss**
and **spin**
and **twist**
...and lots more, too.

Machines make our lives easier.

Many of them look complicated, but they are really made up of many simple machines all working together.

A machine can be as simple as a knife. It may have just one part, like a hammer or a corkscrew. Or it may have several parts that work together. We call many of the simplest machines "tools."

Let's find out more about simple machines....

Six Simple Machines

Did you know that there are just six simple machines? Each one works in a different way. Some move, or help us move around. Others make lifting and pulling easier.

Some simple machines, such as the lever, have just one part that moves. When you use a lever, such as a curved iron bar, to move heavy things, you jam one end under the heavy object and press down on the other end. Presto! The heavy object is lifted up.

Twice as Simple

Other simple machines are made up of two or more parts. A wheel and axle is made up of a wheel and a rod that passes through its center. A wheel and axle helps us move ourselves and other things around.

There are six kinds of simple machines:

1. The **pulley** helps lift heavy loads.

2. The **lever** helps lift or move things.

3. The **ramp** helps things move or slide up and down.

5. The **wedge** cuts and splits.

4. The **screw** turns and lifts.

6. The **wheel and axle** makes it easy to push or pull loads.

The Pulley

1. Many years ago, when people needed to lift a heavy object and place it somewhere else, they had a real problem. There were no machines like we have today to help them do this.

2. Of course, they used muscle power—lots and lots of people all heaving together...

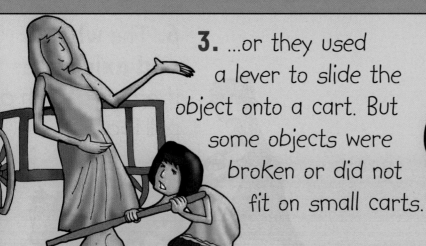

3. ...or they used a lever to slide the object onto a cart. But some objects were broken or did not fit on small carts.

4. A better way was to sling a rope over the branch of a tree and use it to pull the object into position.

5. To make the rope slide easily, a grooved wheel was attached to the branch. The rope was threaded into the groove, and one end was tied to the object.

6. The other end was pulled. The pulley helped lift the load more easily as the weight was taken by the wheel and spread down the length of the rope. The load could then be lowered safely into the cart.

How a Pulley Works

A pulley is a simple machine made up of a wheel, an axle, and a piece of cord or rope.

The wheel of the pulley has a groove cut into its rim where the cord fits. The axle holds the wheel in place and allows it to turn freely. Some pulleys are fitted with just a rope. For heavy jobs, steel cord is needed. One end of the cord is attached to the object that has to be lifted. The other end is used to pull the object up.

The pull is called the **force**, or effort.

The object you want to lift is called the load.

The Lever

A lever is a simple machine that is used to lift or move heavy objects.

A lever can be a bar, a rod, or a flat object such as a board. The main part is called the **arm**. The lever also has a support in the middle or at the end, called the **fulcrum**.

The ancient Egyptians knew how to use a lever to help them do heavy lifting.

A Lever That Raises Water

1. The Nile River flows through much of Egypt, carrying water to the fields nearby. The ancient Egyptians used a lever to lift water out of the Nile River.

2. When the water was low in the river, the farmer could not reach it. How could he raise water to **irrigate** his crops?

Lever Power

A lever has three parts: an arm, a fulcrum, and a load. Look at the man using a plank to lift water. Can you see the lever parts? Like all machines, a lever needs power before it can do its work. Who is powering the lever?

The stone under the plank is the fulcrum.

The man provides the power.

The plank is the arm.

The water in the bucket is called the load.

3. He needed to dip a bucket in the water and raise it. What could he use to make it easy?

4. He used a lever with a raised fulcrum in the middle. At one end of its arm he hung the bucket. A weight, together with muscle-power at the other end, lowered and raised the load.

arm

fulcrum

power

load

11

A Ramp to Build a Monument

1. A builder had a good design for a new tall monument. But his plans meant laying large stone blocks on top of tall, upright pillars.

2. This meant he must raise the huge blocks of stone to a great height. How would he be able to do this? Even if all the builders stood on each other's shoulders, they wouldn't be tall enough.

3. The stones were just too heavy for his team to lift.

4. Then he had an idea. It would mean sliding the stones up a slope.

5. He would pile earth to form a sloping ramp. Then the team could push and pull the stones a little at a time until they reached the right level.

The Inclined Plane

A ramp is also called an inclined plane, which means a flat surface on a **slope**. The ramp is a simple machine that makes lifting things easier.

Lifting something very heavy can be difficult. A ramp makes it easier by allowing you to slide an object along and upward a little at a time, until it has reached the right height.

The Screw

A screw is a simple machine that uses twisting power to raise things, such as water. It is also used to fasten things together.

A screw is shaped like a cylinder but without smooth sides. Instead, a ridge, called a thread, runs up and around it. The ridge acts like a ramp.

A Screw That Lifts Water

1. Archimedes watched men filling their buckets with water and then carrying them to the irrigation ditch.

2. The crops were thirsty, and watering them this way would take a long time. Surely, he thought, there must be a better way to bring water to the dry crops.

Archimedes' Screw

Archimedes was a Greek **mathematician** who lived more than 2,000 years ago. He worked in Egypt, where he invented the screw to help raise water for irrigation. Today we call the screw an Archimedes' screw.

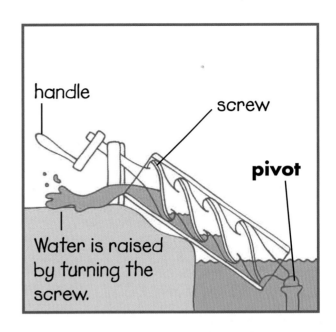

handle

screw

pivot

Water is raised by turning the screw.

3. He knew that many farmers in Egypt used the traditional shadoof— a water-lifting machine that relied on a lever. But even this was hard work, and it took ages! Then Archimedes remembered the screw. Its thread would work like a long, winding ramp, a kind of circular staircase.

4. Twisting the screw would draw the water up its thread.

5. So he placed the screw in a tube and twisted the screw around and around to raise water.

The Wedge

A wedge is a simple machine that is used to cut or split things. A knife is a kind of wedge. So is an axe or the sharp tip of a spear.

A wedge is made from a block of hard material such as iron, steel, or even really tough wood. It is sharpened at one end to make a cutting edge, or blade. The blade is used for cutting or splitting. The downward force of an axe blade can split wood.

The sharp tip of a spear is a kind of wedge.

A Wedge That Was Used to Hunt Lions

1. The villager was unhappy. A lion was catching the wild animals in the area.

2. The villager hunted these animals for food by chasing them into pits or over a cliff. But the lion was eating everything in sight. The villager was getting hungry.

3. He needed a weapon to chase away the lion. But what would *be* frightening enough to scare the beast? He had to *be* able to throw the weapon from a distance. He didn't want to get too close!

4. He sharpened a hard stone to form a cutting blade sharp enough to cut the lion's skin.

5. He attached his sharp wedge to a long stick to make a spear. Now he was ready to hunt.

The Wheel and Axle

A wheel and axle is a simple machine that allows a wheel to turn freely while attached to something else, such as a cart or another wheel.

It is made up of a wheel with a hole, or hub, in the middle. The rod that sticks through the hole is the axle.

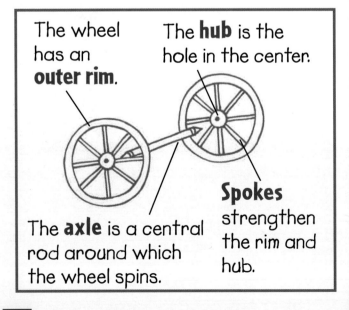

The wheel has an **outer rim**.

The **hub** is the hole in the center.

The **axle** is a central rod around which the wheel spins.

Spokes strengthen the rim and hub.

1. Long ago, people used to spin yarn using the wool sheared from sheep. The wool was fluffy.

2. It had to be washed and combed into strands.

3. But it was still no use until it had been twisted into yarn. Turning wool into yarn required skill!

A Wheel and Axle That Spins Yarn

4. The traditional way of making yarn and winding it onto a **spindle** was long, hard work.

5. What if a wheel could turn the spindle?

6. The wheel could be attached to a foot pedal. The peddling action could then turn the spindle at greater speed.

7. Enough yarn would be produced to weave a cloak.

Simple Machines at Work

Often we can use many simple machines at the same time to do a job such as repairing a car.

In a garage repair shop, mechanics use a wedge, a pulley, a ramp, a wheel-and-axle, and a lever.

Can you spot the simple machines and the job they are helping the mechanics do?

Using a pulley, one or two people can pull the heavy engine out of the car.

Imagine not having wheels on a car! It wouldn't go very far.

A ramp can be used to safely raise the heavy car off the floor.

Screws are used to hold the exhaust pipe tightly in place.

Using a **crowbar** as a lever, a mechanic can get a wheel off a car.

What Powers Machines?

Even if it's just a simple machine you are using, it must move in order to do its work. But it can't move without **energy**. Energy provides the power that makes things move or do work.

A machine needs energy to do work, just as you do. Energy comes from different sources, such as gasoline, coal, natural gas, food—and even you.

A bellows is made up of two levers working together. The air that is blown out provides oxygen to make a fire burn hotter.

This biker pushes the pedals of his bike to turn the wheels. Many machines will move only if you provide the energy to power them!

Energy for Power

The amount of work a machine does in a given time is called power. Energy is needed to do the work that makes the power.

Water and wind are sources of energy that are all around us.

fuel power

human power

steam power

electrical power

solar power

water power

wind power

Machines move in many different ways and use different kinds of energy to do work.

23

Simple Machines in the Home

They often seem so simple that we forget just how important simple machines and tools are. But we owe a lot to the clever people who first developed them, because tools make life much easier for us today. They even help us relax at home!

Tasks that we couldn't do at all, or ones that would have taken lots of people to do, can now be done by just a few of us—or by one person alone!

Staircases are ramps with steps that make it easier for us to get in or out of our homes.

Simple screws, as well as nuts and bolts, can be used to make furniture, hang pictures on the wall, or attach things to one another.

This door handle is a kind of lever and wheel-and-axle combined.

Our knives and forks are wedges that help us eat our food.

This type of latch is made of two levers working together.

Two Machines Together

Sometimes, Two Simple Machines Are Better Than One!

Often, a really helpful machine, such as a pair of scissors, is made of two simple machines working together. The machines work like a team to do a special kind of job.

A Corkscrew

This corkscrew is made up of two levers attached to a screw. When it is twisted, the screw part is pulled down into the cork and the levers are pushed up.

When the levers are pressed down they pull the screw, along with the cork, out of the bottle.

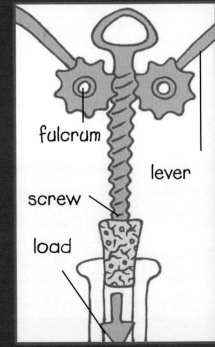

fulcrum

lever

screw

load

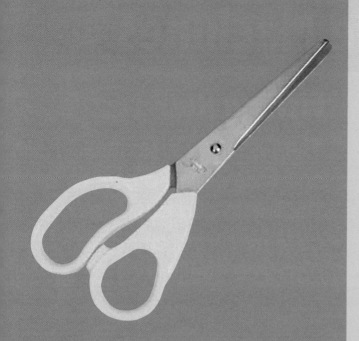

Scissors

A pair of scissors is actually two simple machines. Each blade is a wedge. The two wedges joined together make a lever. The lever action gives the scissors even more power for cutting.

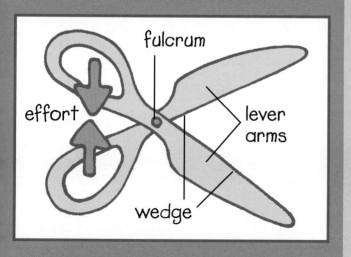

effort

fulcrum

lever arms

wedge

Wheelbarrow

The wheel and axle part of the wheelbarrow makes this machine easy to push. The container and handles are attached to the axle to make a lever. This makes lifting the full wheelbarrow much easier.

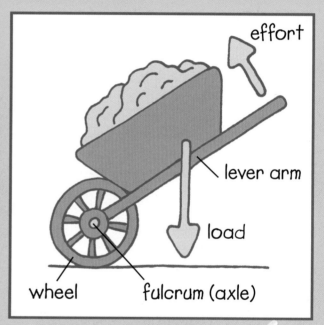

effort

lever arm

load

wheel

fulcrum (axle)

Fun With Simple Machines

Simple machines don't just make life easier. They can be fun, too. Here are some of the fun things that simple machines allow us to do.

Fishing Rod

The fishing rod uses a wheel and axle called a reel to let the line in and out. It also acts as a kind of pulley as the line is pulled in.

Skateboarding

Skateboarding and snowboarding wouldn't be half as much fun if you only had a flat surface to skate on. The **inclined plane** lets you speed down a slope and up the other side, so you can do lots of stunts on the move.

A Lever for Throwing

Parts of the body work like simple machines. We use them to help us exercise and move. When you throw a ball, your elbow and wrist act as levers. The muscles make the levers work. Of course, the bigger your muscles, the more power you have to work the levers.

Bicycle Brakes

The brakes on a bike are operated by a lever on the handlebars. Imagine how hard it would be if you had to pull the brake line with your bare hands—and steer at the same time!

Bow and Arrow

The arrow that an archer shoots is tipped with an arrowhead. The arrowhead is actually a very pointed wedge that cuts easily into its target by splitting it apart.

Wheels

Wheels were a great invention because they made transportation easier. But they also make fun things possible—such as racing **vehicles** with wheels.

Simple Machines Quiz

1. What sort of simple machine do your wrist and your elbow work like?

2. What simple machine did Archimedes invent?

3. What part of a pulley is the object that is lifted?

4. Would you use a pulley or a wedge to chop down a tree?

5. What is the name of the support in the middle, or at the end, of a lever?

6. Until the spinning wheel was invented, how did people turn the spindle to make yarn?

7. What do you need to provide the power to make machines work?

8. How many simple machines does a wheelbarrow use?

9. What simple machines make a door handle?

10. Name two energy sources that are environmentally friendly.

1. A lever 2. The Archimedes' screw 3. The load 4. A wedge 5. The fulcrum 6. By hand 7. You need energy 8. Two 9. A wheel-and-axle and a lever 10. Wind and water

Glossary

arm: the long, straight, or flat part of a lever

crowbar: a metal bar used as a lever to pry things apart

energy: a source of power, such as heat or electricity, that is necessary to make things work

force: the effort that is used to pull or lift something

fulcrum: a point used to support a lever; the spot on which a lever pivots or turns

inclined plane: any surface that lies at an angle to another surface; a ramp

irrigation: (in farming) system that brings water to dry land through the use of ditches, pipes, tunnels, or other artificial methods, including man-made streams

mathematician: an expert in mathematics, the science of numbers and the measurement of shapes and distances

pivot: a point or some part of a structure upon which other parts rotate, turn, or swing. A pivot can act as a fulcrum if it gives support to a lever

slope: a surface, such as a ramp or an inclined plane, that is flat and tilts at an angle to another surface

spindle: a thin rod on which yarn or some other fabric is spun and wound, either by hand or on a machine

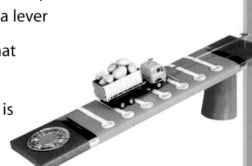

vehicles: machines, such as cars, trucks, or buses, that are driven by a motor and used to transport people or goods from one place to another

Index

ancient Egypt 10, 15
Archimedes' screw 15
arm 10, 11, 27
arrowhead 29
axle 9, 18, 27
bicycle 22, 29
bow and arrow 29
brake 29
cart 8, 9
corkscrew 4, 26
crane 4, 8
crowbar 21
door handle 25
effort 9, 27
electricity 23
energy 22, 23, 28
fishing rod 28
force 9
forklift 8
fuel 23
fulcrum 10, 11, 26, 27
garage 20

hammer 4
hub 18
inclined plane 13, 28
irrigation 14, 15
knife 4, 16, 25
latch 25
lever 4, 6, 7, 10, 11, 15, 20, 21, 22, 25, 26, 27, 28
load 6, 7, 9, 11, 27
muscle 8, 11, 28
pedal 19, 22
pivot 15
pulley 6, 8, 9, 20, 28
ramp 7, 13, 14, 15, 20, 21, 24
rod 6, 10, 28
rope 9
scissors 27
screw 7, 14, 15, 21, 25, 26
shadoof 15
skateboarding 28
slope 13, 28
snowboarding 28

spin 18
spindle 19
spinning wheel 18
spring 23
steam 23
thread 4, 14, 15
tools 4
water 10, 11, 14, 15, 23
wedge 7, 16, 17, 20, 25, 27, 29
wheel 9, 18, 27, 29
wheel and axle 6, 7, 9, 18, 19, 20, 25, 27, 28
wheelbarrow 27
wind 23
yarn 18, 19